W9-ADO-668

ESSENTIAL LIBRARY OF THE
INFORMATION AGE

BOOK BANNING

AND OTHER FORMS OF
CENSORSHIP

by Carolee Laine

CONTENT CONSULTANT

Dr. Caren J. Town
Professor of English
Georgia Southern University

DANVILLE PUBLIC LIBRARY
Danville, Indiana

Essential Library

An Imprint of Abdo Publishing | abdopublishing.com

abdopublishing.com

Published by Abdo Publishing, a division of ABDO, PO Box 398166, Minneapolis, Minnesota 55439. Copyright © 2017 by Abdo Consulting Group, Inc. International copyrights reserved in all countries. No part of this book may be reproduced in any form without written permission from the publisher. Essential Library™ is a trademark and logo of Abdo Publishing.

Printed in the United States of America, North Mankato, Minnesota
052016
092016

THIS BOOK CONTAINS
RECYCLED MATERIALS

Cover Photo: Maksym Sokolov/Shutterstock Images
Interior Photos: iStockphoto, 5, 29, 64; Sean Pavone/Shutterstock Images, 8; Trevor Hunt/ iStockphoto, 12; Jeff Gentner/AP Images, 15; Universal History Archive/Getty Images, 16; Neil Jacobs/Getty Images, 21; AS400 DB/Corbis, 23; Bernard Thomas/The Herald-Sun/AP Images, 25; Kathy Willens/AP Images, 27; LM Otero/AP Images, 30; Bettmann/Corbis, 33, 37; Alan Diaz/AP Images, 35; Marc Golden/The Gadsden Times/AP Images, 41; Tim Boyle/Getty Images, 43; Lefteris Pitarakis/AP Images, 45; Andrew Milligan/PA Wire/AP Images, 51; Ron Edmonda/AP Images, 54; Dan Loh/AP Images, 57; Charles Bertram/Lexington Herald-Leader/MCT/Getty Images, 59, 62; Ted S. Warren/AP Images, 66; Swen Pförtner/picture-alliance/dpa/AP Images, 69; Education Images/ UIG/Getty Images, 73; AP Images, 77; Philippe Lopez/AFP/Getty Images, 79; Shizuo Kambayashi/AP Images, 83; Kyodo/AP Images, 87; Jiao Zi/Imaginechina/AP Images, 89; Imaginechina/AP Images, 90; Gurinder Osan/AP Images, 93; Eduardo Munoz/Reuters, 97; Damian Dovarganes/AP Images, 98

Editor: Arnold Ringstad
Series Designer: Craig Hinton

Publisher's Cataloging in Publication Data

Names: Laine, Carolee, author.
Title: Book banning and other forms of censorship / by Carolee Laine.
Description: Minneapolis, MN : Abdo Publishing, [2017] | Series: Essential library of the information age | Includes bibliographical references and index.
Identifiers: LCCN 2015960308 | ISBN 9781680782837 (lib. bdg.) | ISBN 9781680774726 (ebook)
Subjects: LCSH: Censorship--Juvenile literature. | Challenged books--Juvenile literature. | Prohibited books--Juvenile literature.
Classification: DDC 363--dc23
LC record available at http://lccn.loc.gov/2015960308

CONTENTS

CHAPTER 1

WHAT IS CENSORSHIP?

At the beginning of the 2015 school year, a school in Nashville, Tennessee, became the center of a controversy. A parent complained to a school board member about *City of Thieves*, a book assigned as required reading for seventh-grade students. The parent criticized the language in the book as offensive and inappropriate. The school board member agreed and brought the complaint to the attention of Nashville school district officials.

Written by David Benioff, *City of Thieves* is a work of historical fiction set in Leningrad, a city in the former Soviet Union, during World War II (1939–1945). It recounts the adventures of two teenage boys during the German military's brutal siege of the city. A *Library Journal* review says the book "deserves a bright spotlight in most libraries to attract readers young and old to its compelling pages."[1] Some Nashville school officials questioned whether seventh graders could handle the mature content of the book.

Ravi Gupta, the head of the school, defended *City of Thieves* as an appropriate choice for seventh-grade students who attend one of the highest performing schools in the city. He praised the

School libraries are a key battleground in modern disputes over censorship.

book and supported putting it in the school library. To answer concerns about offensive language, Gupta explained that school staff had already edited out curse words and mature subject matter from the original book. Students were reading a bowdlerized version with objectionable content removed.

This information added a new dimension to the controversy. The National Coalition Against Censorship (NCAC) criticized the school's action as "a particularly disturbing form of censorship."[2] The NCAC strongly urged teachers to stop using the edited version of *City of Thieves* and provide the book to students as the author intended it.

OFFENSIVE BOOKS

The controversy in Nashville raised questions that have been debated for many years: Who decides what is appropriate for students to read? Should language that some people consider offensive be removed from a book?

In 1977, a similar situation occurred in Chelsea, Massachusetts. A parent complained about offensive language in a book his daughter had borrowed from the high school library. The book, titled *Male and Female Under 18*, was an anthology that contained many writings by young people. It included the poem "The City, to a Young Girl," in which the 15-year-old writer describes a girl's feelings about being taunted by men on the street.

The parent's complaint touched off a heated debate. On one side of the issue were the school committee and some parents who wanted to protect students from writing they considered offensive. On the other side were the school librarian and teachers who wanted to provide students with a wide variety of uncensored reading materials.

The committee chairman read the poem and decided the language was "filthy" and "offensive."[4] Without reading any other part of the anthology, he recommended removing the book from the school library. Later, the committee said the book could be

The argument in Chelsea went to the US District Court for the District of Massachusetts.

used if the poem were cut out. In a series of special meetings of the school committee and over the course of several editorials in the city newspaper, the debate grew heated. The committee discussed reassigning the librarian and seeking the resignations of teachers who defended the poem. The matter ended up in federal court.

The Right to Read Defense Committee, a group formed by the school librarian and others, asked the court to have the anthology returned to the library. This group claimed the removal of the book violated the First Amendment rights of students, teachers, and library staff. The school committee defended its action by claiming that removing a book from the library was within its authority to determine the curriculum of the school.

The First Amendment to the US Constitution reads, in part, "Congress shall make no law . . . abridging the freedom of speech, or of the press."[6]

The interpretation of this short clause has been the subject of much debate in the more than 200 years since the Bill of Rights was added to the Constitution. The Supreme Court has interpreted speech and press to mean many forms of expression, including talking, writing, publishing, and using the Internet. However, there are some exceptions to the right to free speech. Supreme Court decisions have determined that the following kinds of expression are not protected by the First Amendment:

>> fighting words, which inflict injury or cause an act of violence

>> damaging lies about a person

>> words or images that are considered legally obscene

The decisions in a court case often rely on precedents, or previous decisions in similar cases. In *Presidents Council District 25 v. Community School Board No. 25* (1972), a federal court had upheld a school board's right to remove books from a high school library. The judge found no violation of First Amendment rights and ruled that the right to decide which books are shelved in a school library belonged to the elected members of the school board. In *Minarcini v. Strongsville City School District* (1976), a different federal court had ruled that books removed by a school board had to be returned to the library shelves. The judge ruled that once a school board had chosen books for students' use, it could not place conditions on their use solely because of the social or political tastes of school board members. The US District Court of Massachusetts would have to decide which precedent applied to the Chelsea case.

THE COURT'S DECISION

In *Right to Read Defense Committee of Chelsea v. School Committee of the City of Chelsea*, Judge Joseph L. Tauro handed down a decision defending a student's right to read. He ruled that the school committee had neither the right to bowdlerize the anthology by removing the poem nor the power to exercise censorship by removing the book from the library. His decision states:

If this work may be removed by a committee hostile to its language and theme, then the precedent is set for removal of any other work. The prospect of successive school committees sanitizing the school of views divergent from their own is alarming. . . . What is at stake here is the right to read and be exposed to controversial thoughts and language—a valuable right subject to First Amendment protection.[7]

Tauro's decision became an important milestone in the ongoing debate over censorship. In the decision, Tauro acknowledges "The City, to a Young Girl" is not a polite poem, and its language is tough. He says its vivid street language is "legitimately offensive to some, but certainly not to everyone."[8]

People will always disagree about what is offensive, and they have a right to their opinions. People on both sides of an issue have strong reasons for their opinions. Controversy arises when differing opinions about what is offensive lead to censorship.

DEFINING CENSORSHIP

> **"** The library is a mighty resource in the marketplace of ideas. There a student can literally explore the unknown. . . . The student who discovers the magic of the library is on the way to a life-long experience of self-education and enrichment. **"** [9]
>
> —Judge Joseph L. Tauro

The word *censorship* refers to the suppression of information. It occurs when the government, church authorities, special-interest groups, or individuals impose their values on other people by limiting what others may read, write, hear, or see. Censorship affects all forms of media, including books, magazines, newspapers, movies, television, radio, photographs, art, music, video games, and the Internet.

Censorship can occur at different times and in different ways. A publisher might require a writer to change or delete parts of a book because some people could find them objectionable. A museum might refuse to exhibit art that someone could consider offensive. The removal of books from a library or bookstore because some people object to them is another form of censorship.

Because of people's First Amendment rights, one group of people may not, on the basis of their personal morals or beliefs,

Documents are sometimes censored by blacking out parts of the text.

restrict what information should be available to others. People cannot impose their views of what is appropriate or offensive on everyone else. People cannot pressure libraries to remove materials they consider objectionable so that no one else has a chance to

> Expurgating [removing words from] a book is a particularly disturbing form of censorship since it not only suppresses specific content deemed 'objectionable,' but it also does violence to the work as a whole by removing material that the author thought integral. [10]
>
> —National Coalition Against Censorship

read the materials and make up their own minds about them.

Does freedom of expression mean there are no limits to what people can write or say? Do schools and parents have the right to decide what is appropriate for children to read? Who decides what is objectionable? These questions have been debated in US courts since the Bill of Rights was added to the Constitution in 1791, but the history of censorship dates back much further than that.

CHAPTER 2

BANNED!

Some high school students in Florida were surprised when a book they had read as a required summer assignment was removed from the library two weeks before school started. In New Mexico, a popular graphic novel was removed from a school library and kept in the superintendent's desk. Students needed their parents' permission to read the book. In Iowa, an award-winning book was pulled from middle school classrooms. These incidents all happened in 2015. Book banning, or prohibiting the reading of books, is as recent as today's headlines and as old as the written word.

BOOK BANNING THROUGHOUT HISTORY

In ancient times, all books were handwritten. This greatly limited their number, making it easy for authorities to restrict access to them. The invention of the printing press in the mid-1400s greatly increased the number of available books. Governments found it more challenging to prevent people from reading books. At the same time, censors became more organized.

During the 1500s, governments in Germany, France, and England established official censorship systems. Germany

A West Virginia high school student shows two books banned by a local school following parent complaints.

THE #1 NEW YORK TIMES BESTSELLING AUTHOR
PAT CONROY
BEACH
Now a Major Motion Picture Starring
BARBRA STREISAND and NICK NOLTE
THE TWO MILLION-COPY
BESTSELLER
THE PRINCE OF TIDES
PAT CONROY

People burned books by religious opponents in Germany in the 1500s.

established a censorship office, and town officials censored publications they considered dangerous. England's licensing system required printers to submit all manuscripts to Church of England authorities for approval. The French king Francis I prohibited the printing of books.

In 1559, the Roman Catholic Church published the *Index,* a list of forbidden books. The original purpose of the *Index* was to guide censors in their decisions about which books to prohibit. It later became a guide about books the Catholic Church considered inappropriate for its members. The Catholic Church continued to publish the *Index* until 1966.

Burning has been an effective way of destroying books throughout history. The practice traveled to America with English colonists in the 1600s and became firmly established in the United States. Puritan authorities in Massachusetts confiscated a religious pamphlet, which was condemned by the General Court. The public burning of this pamphlet in the Boston marketplace in 1650 is considered the first book burning in America.

> " We all know that books burn, yet we have the greater knowledge that books cannot be killed by fire. " [2]
>
> —President Franklin D. Roosevelt

Anthony Comstock, who founded the New York Society for the Suppression of Vice in the 1870s, was perhaps the most famous book burner in US history. The logo for Comstock's organization featured an image of a man tossing books into a fire. Comstock lobbied Congress and succeeded in getting a law passed that banned the mailing of materials considered to be indecent. As a special agent of the US Post Office, Comstock was able to use that law to confiscate printed works. Between 1874 and 1915, he destroyed an estimated 15 short tons (13.6 metric tons) of books he considered objectionable.[1]

BANNED IN BOSTON

The organization that became known as the Watch and Ward Society was founded in the late 1800s but reached the height of its power in Boston in the 1920s. This group of private citizens included members from Boston's most prominent families. The mission of the Watch and Ward Society was to rid the city of "immoral" books. This gave rise to the phrase "Banned in Boston."

The society determined which books could be sold in Boston, so Bostonians began traveling outside the city to buy books they wanted to read. Boston booksellers began to complain about the loss of business. The efforts of the Watch and Ward Society backfired, because they actually boosted sales of the books they banned. Author Upton Sinclair stated, "I would rather be banned in Boston than read anywhere else because when you are banned in Boston, you are read everywhere else."[3]

Book banning in the United States continued in the 1900s. During the 1920s, private organizations, such as the Watch and Ward Society, sponsored book bans. Parents objected to some of the books their children read in school, and school boards removed books based on parents' complaints. Other groups, such as the American Civil Liberties Union (ACLU), challenged censorship laws. Several notable US Supreme Court cases and federal court cases defined freedom of expression under the First Amendment. Court decisions upheld the right to read freely and established guidelines for protecting that right. Despite those guidelines, attempts to ban or restrict access to books have continued into the 2000s.

WHY BOOKS ARE CHALLENGED

A challenge is a complaint against a book in a school library or a public library and an attempt to prevent people from checking it out, while a ban is the removal of a book to outright prohibit its use. Challenges are based on the objections of a person or a group. They are usually made with the intention of protecting others, especially children, from ideas or information the challenger finds difficult or inappropriate. In some cases, challengers try to suppress anything that conflicts with their own beliefs. If challengers are successful, materials are banned, or removed from access by others.

The Office for Intellectual Freedom (OIF), a division of the American Library Association that compiles data about challenged books, reported more than 5,000 official challenges in the United States between 2000 and 2009. In addition, the OIF estimates up to 85 percent of book challenges remain unreported.[4] Most challenges come from the parents of students. The list of challenged titles varies from year to year. People give many reasons for their objections to books.

OFFICE FOR INTELLECTUAL FREEDOM

Intellectual freedom is a person's right to information from all points of view, without restriction, even if the information is offensive to others. The Office for Intellectual Freedom (OIF) protects that right in libraries. It educates the public about the importance of intellectual freedom in libraries. It also maintains a database to record and report challenges to library materials across the country. The OIF provides training for librarians to help them handle challenges to materials in their collections. It also provides financial assistance to librarians who have been fired because of an intellectual freedom dispute.

BOOK BURNING— EXTREME CENSORSHIP

In December 2001, international media attention focused on Alamogordo, New Mexico. The event that gained such attention was the burning of books from the popular Harry Potter series. Headlines in the United States and in the United Kingdom, home of series author J. K. Rowling, featured the story.

Harry Potter, the main character in the books, is a boy who attends a wizard school. Harry battles the forces of evil through the use of magical powers. The pastor of a local church in Alamogordo was among critics who denounced the books for promoting witchcraft. He preached a sermon in which he stated, "The Potter books present witchcraft as a generally positive practice."[5] This idea conflicted with the beliefs of his church.

The pastor said he had never read any of the Harry Potter novels, but he had researched their contents. The pastor's sermon was followed by a book burning in which several Harry Potter books and other works the pastor considered objectionable were thrown on a bonfire. Other items destroyed included horror novels by Stephen King, Ouija boards supposedly used to talk to the dead, and albums by rock group AC/DC and rapper Eminem.

The December 2001 burning also included other books and games the pastor disliked, including Ouija boards.

While the church group supported the pastor's actions, other members of the community protested nearby. Some wore black witch hats in support of the Potter books. One resident said, "Burning books leads to ignorance, and that's why I'm standing out here. My son loves Harry Potter."[6] Another held a sign comparing the pastor to dictator Adolf Hitler and terrorist leader Osama bin Laden.

In 2012, the Library of Congress created an exhibit called *Books That Shaped America*. The purpose of the exhibit was to celebrate books that "have had a profound effect on American life."[7] The exhibit, according to the Library of Congress, represented the choices of curators and experts from the library, who admitted agonizing over having to limit the list to fit the available exhibition space.

Many of the books featured in the exhibit, such as *Adventures of Huckleberry Finn*, had been banned or challenged. The exhibitors believed books that had been the source of controversy helped shape Americans' views of the world and the world's view of Americans. The *Books That Shaped America* exhibition was intended to spark a national conversation on books and their importance in Americans' lives.

The most common objections are racism, sexual material, offensive language, violence, homosexuality, witchcraft, blasphemous religious views, unpopular political views, and content the challenger believes is unsuitable for a particular age group.

A FREQUENTLY CHALLENGED BOOK

When it was published in 1885, Mark Twain's *Adventures of Huckleberry Finn* caused controversy. After 130 years, it still appears on lists of the most frequently challenged books in the United States. The story takes place in the 1840s. Huck, a white boy who is escaping an abusive father, and Jim, an African-American man who is escaping slavery, travel together down the Mississippi River on a raft.

Adventures of Huckleberry Finn is commonly regarded as one of the greatest novels in American literature.

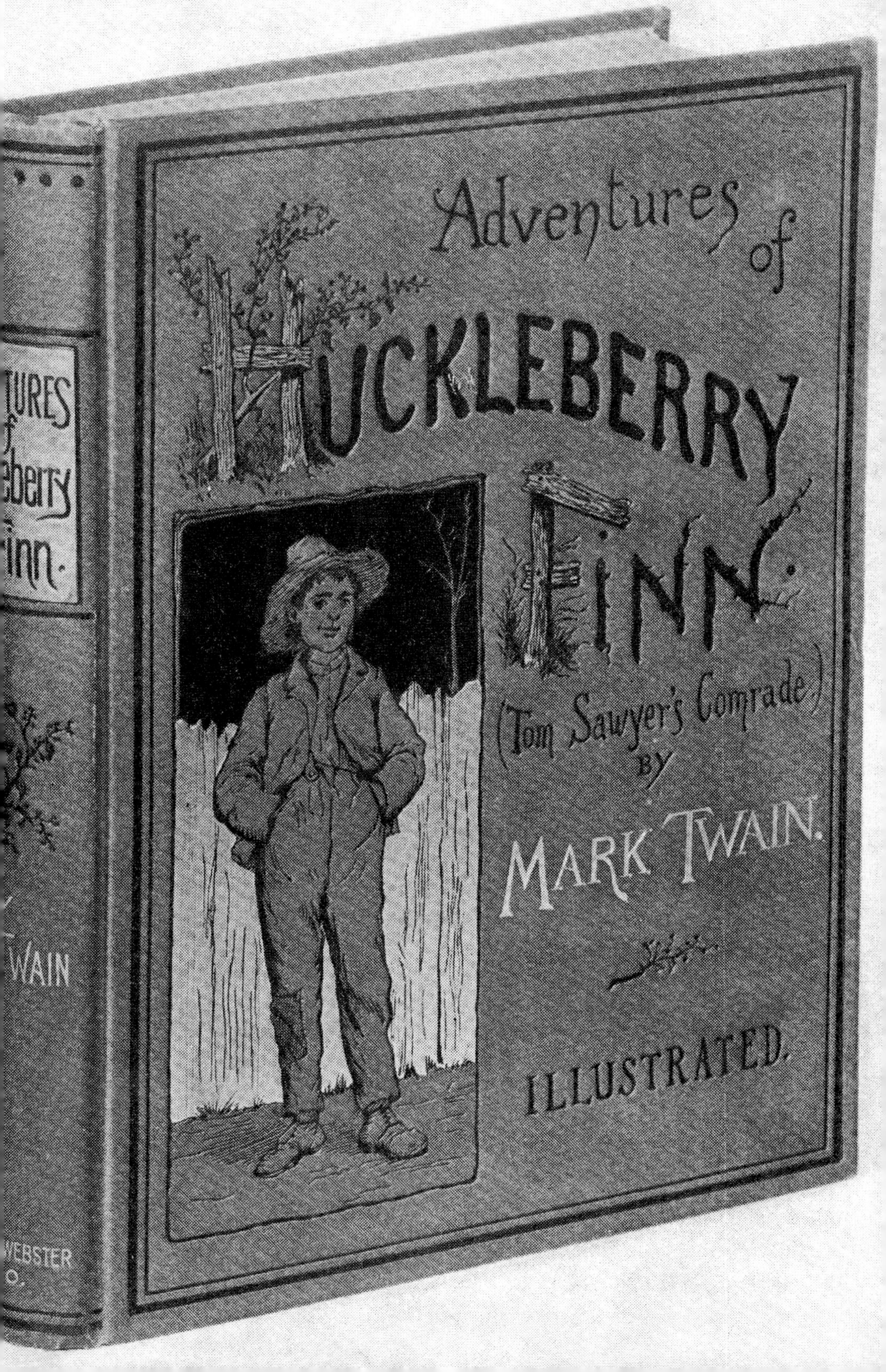
Adventures of
HUCKLEBERRY
FINN.
(Tom Sawyer's Comrade)
BY
MARK TWAIN.
ILLUSTRATED.
TURES
of
leberry
Finn.
TWAIN
WEBSTER
O.

During the last week of September each year since 1982, US libraries and bookstores have celebrated Banned Books Week. The event is sponsored by the American Library Association and several other groups that promote the right to read freely. These groups support the freedom to choose and express opinions, even if the opinions are unpopular. They also believe strongly in making all viewpoints available to anyone who wishes to explore them.

Displays of banned and challenged books draw attention to the problem of censorship. A variety of events encourage readers to discuss the issues and controversies surrounding book challenges and book banning. Banned Books Week celebrates the efforts of librarians, teachers, students, and community members who support the freedom to read. It stresses the importance of making books available to those who wish to read them.

Those who criticize the book find the language offensive. Huck's speech is coarse, and some people feel the book promotes racism through derogatory language and attitudes. Critics also object to Huck's lack of respect for religion and adult authority. They believe the content is inappropriate for children.

Those who defend the book point out that although the language is offensive by today's standards, it accurately portrays the common speech of the time period it represents. They view Huck's friendship with Jim as an attack on racism.

THE RIGHT TO CHOOSE

People who challenge books may not see their actions as censorship. Parents seeking to protect their children from books they consider offensive may feel they have a responsibility to

A school librarian places a book into a cage to make a point about how and why books are challenged.

What's the
difference
between a
challenge and a
banning?

Why are books
challenged?

protect all children. A statement from the American Library Association known as the Library Bill of Rights states that parents have the right and the responsibility to restrict only their own children's access to library resources. Censorship occurs when parent objections restrict everyone's access to materials.

Challenging or banning books also impacts the rights of the authors who wrote them. Robert Cormier, author of the frequently challenged book *We All Fall Down*, states, "I try to write realistic stores about believable people, reflecting the world as it is, not as we wish it to be."[8] Judy Blume, another author whose works have often been challenged, says, "Children have rights, too, and in some places, children are beginning to understand that they have a right to choose what they want to read."[9]

Judy Blume has been writing popular novels since the 1970s.

CHAPTER 3

CENSORSHIP IN SCHOOLS

In the United States, a student in middle school or high school spends approximately 1,000 hours per year in school.[1] What legal principles govern students' rights during this time? In a landmark 1969 Supreme Court decision dealing with First Amendment rights, *Tinker v. Des Moines Independent Community School District*, Justice Abe Fortas stated, "It can hardly be argued that either students or teachers shed their constitutional rights to freedom of speech or expression at the schoolhouse gate."[2]

The First Amendment protects students' rights to freedom of expression. This does not mean, however, that students may say, read, or write anything they choose. School authorities have rights, too. Are school policies a form of censorship? In situations where students' rights conflict with policies established by school authorities, court decisions have provided answers.

THE RIGHT TO LEARN

The goal of the education system in the United States is to prepare students to become informed citizens. To do this, schools must provide exposure to knowledge of every kind. School officials

The limits on free speech in schools have been the subject of many legal disputes over the past several decades.

Textbook choices often attract criticism and controversy.

have the authority and responsibility to accomplish this task. Decisions about curriculum standards, graduation requirements, and standardized testing are made at the state level. These decisions influence the choice of educational materials provided at individual schools.

The selection of textbooks presents unique challenges. Textbooks go through a strict review process before they can be marketed to schools. The National School Boards Association and other professional educators recommend two guidelines for selecting textbooks: the books should have a clear connection to educational goals, and they should meet the needs of the students who will use them. Many states have formal regulations for approving textbooks for use in district classrooms. Some states welcome public input or opposition to proposed selections.

Both federal and state governments give schools money to purchase textbooks approved by state departments of education. The final selection is up to district school boards, and sometimes up to classroom teachers with school board approval.

Conflicts between community values and textbook selection led to heated debates and even violence in the 1970s. For many years, Mel and Norma Gabler, textbook censors in Texas, succeeded in influencing the nationwide textbook market with their particular social and religious ideas. Because Texas is such a large textbook market, many books used nationwide were produced to fit its standards well into the 2000s. The high cost of developing a separate Texas edition of a science or social studies textbook made it easier for publishers to develop one edition that would meet Texas requirements and then market it nationwide.

THE GABLERS

In the early 1960s, Mel and Norma Gabler began a textbook-criticism crusade at their kitchen table in Hawkins, Texas. Their business grew into a corporation—Educational Research Analysts. And their influence grew into a major force for textbook censorship throughout the United States for the next four decades. The Gablers' line-by-line reviews turned up hundreds of factual errors in history textbooks and helped the couple gain credibility with Texas school officials. The Gablers also censored content that did not agree with their personal views. The state of Texas accepted the Gablers' judgments.

TEXTBOOK WARS

Kanawha County, West Virginia, was the site of the nation's most violent protest over textbooks. What became known as the Great Textbook War started in 1974 when the board of education adopted new language arts books for the county's schools. The books reflected state guidelines, which called for multicultural content to expose students to new ideas and different traditions. The books included works by a diverse range of authors, including African Americans, Jews, and other minorities.

One school board member protested the books, which she considered anti-Christian and un-American. Soon she was joined by ministers, community members, and business leaders who wanted the books banned. Protesters formed picket lines around schools and businesses throughout the county. Businesses shut down to avoid the protesters, and bus service stopped.

More than 3,000 coal miners went on strike to protest the textbooks.[3] Members of the hate group the Ku Klux Klan marched on the capitol and burned crosses. The violence included shootings and firebombings. Schools were shut down for four days to protect students and teachers.

Striking coal miners made up one of several groups that ignited the Great Textbook War.

In the end, the school board approved the books, but a conservative school board member, representing the views of the antitextbook protesters, created a series of guidelines for selecting future books. These included requirements such as encouraging loyalty to the United States and representing the ideals of the founders. The school board approved the guidelines. Some of the controversial books the board had approved were placed only in school libraries and required parent permission for student use. Principals had veto power over the use of books in their schools. As a result, many of the controversial books never ended up in classrooms.

THE RIGHT TO PUBLISH

Are student-run newspapers protected by freedom of the press under the First Amendment? It depends. Generally, a school newspaper is considered a nonpublic forum, which means school officials have the right to censor controversial material. However, the censorship must be based on a valid educational reason.

In the 1988 *Hazelwood School District v. Kuhlmeier* decision, the Supreme Court ruled a high school principal did not violate students' rights by removing articles about teen pregnancy and divorce from a school newspaper. The principal's action was based on protecting the privacy of students described in the articles and protecting the school from a possible lawsuit.

In the 2004 *Dean v. Utica Community Schools* decision, a federal court ruled in favor of student journalists who published a story about a lawsuit filed by community residents against the school district. A family that lived near the district's school bus parking lot complained that the buses were left idling for hours. Family members claimed they became ill from breathing the exhaust fumes.

In the school newspaper article, student reporters noted the bus parking lot was also near the high school athletic field and an elementary school playground. School officials refused to comment for the story. The newspaper staff was ordered not to publish it. The court ruled the school's attempt to censor the

Controversy over school newspapers combines questions about freedom of the press and student free speech.

A high school student in Alaska tested the limits of free speech by displaying a banner that promoted the use of illegal drugs. Although the banner was not on school property, it was displayed at a school-sponsored event. The school principal removed the banner and suspended the student. The student sued the school for violating his rights. In the 2007 case *Morse v. Frederick*, the Supreme Court ruled in favor of the school, which had a right to censor speech that conflicted with school antidrug policies.

A senior in Washington State spoke in front of a high school assembly to nominate a classmate for a student government office. His speech was filled with sexual references. The school suspended the student. The student's parents sued the school for violating their son's free speech rights. The case eventually went to the Supreme Court. In the 1986 case *Bethel School District v. Fraser*, the court ruled in favor of the school because the student's speech had caused a disruption and violated the sensibilities of other students.

story was based on a desire to silence a viewpoint with which it disagreed.

THE RIGHT TO SPEAK OUT

In 1965, Mary Beth Tinker was suspended from school for protesting the Vietnam War (1954–1975) by wearing a black armband. In *Tinker v. Des Moines Community School District*, the US Supreme Court upheld Mary Beth's right to protest. The court ruled the armband was a form of symbolic speech. It was a "passive expression of opinion, unaccompanied by any disorder or disturbance," so it was protected under the First Amendment.[4]

A key part of the court's decision states, "Conduct by the student, in class or out of it, which for any reason—whether it stems from time, place, or type of behavior—materially disrupts

The actions of Mary Beth Tinker, *left*, spurred a landmark Supreme Court decision.

classwork or involves substantial disorder or invasion of the rights of others is, of course, not immunized by the constitutional guarantee of freedom of speech."[5] By this decision, the Supreme Court established what has come to be known as the Tinker Test for determining when schools can legally restrict students' freedom of expression. The two criteria for restriction are disrupting the educational process or invading the rights of others.

In more recent times, the Internet has complicated the issue of students' right to speak out. Are Facebook or Twitter posts protected under the First Amendment? In several cases heard in federal or state courts, the *Tinker* decision has been applied. Courts have ruled in favor of students' rights to criticize teachers or school officials as long as the Internet posts did not pose a threat or disrupt the educational process. Courts have supported schools' rights to suspend students if their Internet posts violated another person's rights or disrupted school activities.

THE RIGHT TO READ FREELY

School officials, teachers, and librarians face several challenges in protecting students' right to read freely. Teachers may select books for their classes based on several criteria. They may consider the value of the work, its readability for different groups of students, its appeal to readers, and the message it conveys. Selection is not the same as censorship. Selection is the freedom to choose a book for a particular purpose and group of students. Censorship is deciding not to use a book because it may be objectionable to someone.

> " They are using all the tools available, including online speech, to make a positive contribution. Today, students have more than armbands. "[6]
>
> —Mary Beth Tinker, speaking in 2014

Schools are frequently under pressure to restrict student access to books and other materials that some individual or group finds

> **"** The undoubted freedom to advocate unpopular and controversial views in schools and classrooms must be balanced against society's countervailing interest in teaching students the boundaries of socially appropriate behavior. **"** [7]
>
> —Justice Warren Burger, *Bethel School District v. Fraser*, 1986

objectionable. Most complaints come from concerned parents or other family members who are interested in the well-being of children. The First Amendment protects the right of people to express their concerns. It also protects the right of educators to provide meaningful learning experiences for students and to decide what is appropriate for them. Both sides of the issue are important to understanding the wide range of issues involved in censorship cases.

CHAPTER 4

BOTH SIDES OF THE ISSUE

Censorship is not merely a matter of deciding who is right and who is wrong. The First Amendment protects the freedom to disagree and to challenge the ideas of others. People who challenge books have a legal right to do so. In communities throughout the country, challenges are often made by well-meaning administrators, religious groups, politicians, and parents. They argue for the removal of books they find offensive and believe may be potentially harmful to children or to society.

On the other side of the issue are teachers, librarians, concerned citizens, and students who seek to protect the right to read freely. They argue for access to books that mirror the complicated ideas of the real world. Groups on both sides believe they are doing what is best. Two frequently challenged books, *To Kill a Mockingbird* and *The Kite Runner*, provide an opportunity to examine arguments on both sides of the issue of censorship.

TO KILL A MOCKINGBIRD

Harper Lee's novel *To Kill a Mockingbird* was published in 1960. It won the Pulitzer Prize for Literature, along with many other

School libraries often set up displays to highlight Banned Books Week.

One of the earliest supporters of censorship was the Greek philosopher Plato. In *The Republic*, written in 360 BCE, Plato argues in favor of shielding children from ideas that are "the very opposite of those which we should wish them to have when they are grown up."[1] He proposed that those in charge of children's education should teach only morally uplifting stories. He advocated for the government to appoint censors of literature to ensure only "good" stories were taught to children.

awards. Since the mid-1960s, the book has been read widely in middle school and high school literature classes. It also has appeared frequently on lists of the top ten challenged books of the 2000s.

Scout, the adult narrator in Lee's book, describes events she experienced as a six-year-old girl in a small southern town during the 1930s. Through a child's eyes, the book depicts the attitudes and behaviors of white society in the rural South at the time. Scout experiences violence and hypocrisy as she grows up. She witnesses tolerance as well as prejudice. The story deals with racism, injustice, gender roles, and family values.

Some censors object to profanity and vulgar language in the book. Others say the book promotes racism. Though innocent, a man is convicted of a crime, rape, because he is African American. Parents complain the subject of rape is inappropriate for their children to read about. A parent expressed the following criticism in a letter to a school principal: "I feel the book serves no purpose but to keep racism and separatism alive. . . . We know these feelings of hatred and prejudice are still harbored by some people, but

To Kill a Mockingbird received renewed attention in 2015 when Lee's companion novel, Go Set a Watchman, was published.

should those responsible for our children's education play a part in keeping bigotry, superiority, and hatred alive?"[2]

Defenders praise To Kill a Mockingbird as a realistic portrayal of life in the rural South during the Great Depression. They argue that as the characters gain insights about the issues of racism and injustice, so do the readers. A school superintendent defended the book as "a work of art that clearly confronts racism. The highest result of education is teaching tolerance. This book is unflinching in its condemnation of racial prejudice."[3]

THE KITE RUNNER

Khaled Hosseini's novel *The Kite Runner*, published in 2003, became an international best seller. In 2014, Nobel Peace Prize winner and proponent of universal education Malala Yousafzai named *The Kite Runner* as a book all students should read. It is taught in classrooms around the world. It also became one of the most frequently challenged books in recent history.

Hosseini won a Galaxy British Book Award for *The Kite Runner*.

In 2009, at the age of 11, Malala Yousafzai was blogging in support of girls' rights to education in her native country, Pakistan. As a teenager, she became an outspoken advocate for girls' education. Because of her views, she was shot by the Taliban, a fundamentalist religious group opposed to women's rights, on her way home from school in September 2012. She survived the attack, went to live in the United Kingdom, and gained international recognition for her courage. When Malala was 17 years old, she was awarded the Nobel Peace Prize.

Malala's father said, "I didn't do anything special. As a father, I did one thing. I gave her the right of freedom of expression."[6] Malala continued to exercise that right. However, she became a victim of censorship herself when her book, *I Am Malala*, was banned by schools in Pakistan.

The story's adult narrator, Amir, recalls his experiences as a boy in Kabul, Afghanistan, in the 1970s and early 1980s. The story describes the last peaceful days of the nation's monarchy and the changes that occurred as a result of revolution and an invasion by Russian forces. Amir experiences fierce cruelty, guilt, and redeeming love as he grows up during a difficult time in his country's history. The story deals with friendship, betrayal, prejudice, violence, and the effects of war.

Some censors object to the book's religious viewpoints and offensive language. Many parents believe the description of the rape of a young boy makes the book unfit for children. Defenders of *The Kite Runner* believe the story's

> "A book worthless to me may convey something of value to my neighbor. In the free society to which our Constitution has committed us, it is for each to choose for himself."[7]
>
> —US Supreme Court Justice Potter Stewart, *Ginzburg v. United States*, 1966

themes are universal. Although the sensitive subject matter may not be appropriate for some readers, the book deals with the consequences of choices and the triumph of the human spirit. Teachers also praise the book for providing insights into the history and culture of Afghanistan. A teacher's defense of the book stated, "It is a tale not only of friendship and heartbreak, heroism and cowardice, but also of an Afghanistan that not many of our students can even imagine. . . . *The Kite Runner* is a great book to use in discussions of Afghan culture, class divisions and the importance of friendship."[8]

ARGUMENTS FOR AND AGAINST CENSORSHIP

Many people who favor censorship view books and their characters as possible negative role models. They believe young readers will imitate the behavior they read about in books. Censors seek to protect readers from offensive language, violence, indecency, and lifestyles other than their own by restricting children's access to books that include these aspects of life. Censors challenge books that model what they consider

KIDS' RIGHT TO READ

The Kids' Right to Read Project was started in 2007 by the NCAC and the American Booksellers Foundation for Free Expression. Its purpose is to help people fight book challenges in schools and libraries. The project provides advice and assistance to students and teachers to oppose book banning in communities nationwide. It also publishes educational materials to promote awareness about the right to read. The Kids' Right to Read Project maintains a website with videos and tools for fighting censorship.

PARENTAL RIGHTS

Throughout US history, the Supreme Court has upheld "the liberty of parents to direct the upbringing, education, and care of their children" (*Pierce v. Society of Sisters*, 1925).[9] In the 2000 decision in *Troxel v. Granville*, grandparents petitioned the court for specific visitation rights with their grandchildren. The court ruled in favor of parents' rights to limit visitation of their children with other people. The judge cited a long list of previous cases that "reflect a strong tradition of parental concern for the nurture and upbringing of their children. This primary role of the parents in the upbringing of their children is now established beyond debate as an enduring American tradition."[10]

In 2005, however, a federal district court ruled that parental rights to direct children's education end at the threshold of the school door. Parents may make reasonable choices for their child, such as keeping the child out of classes the parents find objectionable. However, the court ruling indicates that parents do not have a fundamental constitutional right to dictate the curriculum at the public school to which they have chosen to send their children.

Some groups have proposed a Parental Rights Amendment to the Constitution. The law would, in part, give parents the right to "make reasonable choices within the public schools" for their children.[11] Opponents see this as a dangerous threat to the public education system.

inappropriate moral behavior. They promote the reading of books that describe the world as they believe it should be.

People who oppose censorship, such as Peruvian novelist Mario Vargas Llosa, believe restricting access to books limits readers' abilities to become effective independent thinkers. Teachers believe censorship prevents them from using their knowledge and experience to choose books that engage students in meaningful reading. People who support the right to read freely believe exploring diverse ideas and lifestyles promotes tolerance.

> **"** Either a rigorous censorship of the mass media, in conformity with responsible republican government, with censors known to all and operating under law, or an accelerating descent into barbarism and the destruction, sooner or later, of free society itself. **"** [12]
>
> —David Lowenthal, political scientist and constitutional scholar

They support the reading of books that reveal the realities of life in order to prepare readers to meet their own challenges.

CHAPTER 5

THE INTERNET AND FREEDOM OF EXPRESSION

A blog called *Never Seconds*, written by a nine-year-old girl in western Scotland, gained worldwide attention in 2012. Martha Payne posted photographs of lunches being served in the public school she attended. She complained the portions were small and the food was not very tasty. Martha's blog received a lot of attention—more than one million viewers within a few weeks. It even resulted in school-food reform in the district. The blog also raised money for a local charity called Mary's Meals, which funded school lunches for people living in poverty in Africa.

Then school officials told Martha she could no longer take pictures of school lunches to post on her blog. National newspapers had picked up the story, and the school was receiving unwanted negative attention. Later that day, Martha posted that she would shut down her blog.

The school district's attempt to censor Martha's blog had some surprising results. Within a few hours, Martha received public

Martha Payne's blog demonstrated the power of the Internet to bring attention to issues.

NeverSeconds

One primary school pupil's daily dose of school dinners.

Monday, 17 September 2012

Hi Veg, and friends of NeverSeconds!

We are so happy to participate in your Around-the-World Lunch Tour. We are in kindergarten and our classroom is called JAM (how perfect is that, better yet on toast). Which JAM is your favorite? (Strawberry!-Veg)

We thought would be nice to start by sharing a video that our school principal, Jackie, made: Greeting the World in Peace. In the video, Jackie takes a few moments to consider the common theme behind so many of the diverse greetings people use around the world:

Greeting the world in peace - Jackie Jenkins   Share   ⬇ More info

iceland   LONDON

Blog Archive

September (17)

August (35)

July (40)

June (21)

May (17)

April (1)

About Me

⬛ VEG

My dad says I should call myself Veritas Ex Gustu, truth from tasting in Latin but who knows Latin? You can call me Veg.

View my complete profile

Mary's Meals

MARY'S MEALS

My JustGiving page for Mary's Meals

MacBook Pro

support from around the world. Her number of blog followers increased dramatically, and donations to Mary's Meals exceeded all expectations. School officials lifted the ban.

ONLINE CENSORSHIP

The phenomenon experienced by the school district that censored Martha's blog is informally known as the Streisand effect. The name comes from a situation involving singer Barbra Streisand. It means that an attempt to ban information on the Internet has the unintended effect of making the information more widely known.

In 1995, less than one percent of the world's population had access to the Internet. In 2015, almost 50 percent of the world's population—more than three billion people—were online.[1] This phenomenal growth of the Internet raised many questions about censorship. The basic issue for the Internet is similar to the issue faced by other forms of expression. The right to free speech must be balanced with concerns about protecting

STREISAND EFFECT

In 2003, singer and actor Barbra Streisand sued the California Coastal Records Project. This company maintains online photographic records of much of the California coastline. Streisand claimed her privacy had been invaded because photos posted to the company's website showed her cliffside home in Malibu. As a result of the publicity over the lawsuit, hundreds of thousands of people visited the website to view Streisand's home. The photos received far more attention than they would have otherwise. This phenomenon, in which attempting to censor the Internet results in additional attention, is now called the Streisand effect.

children from inappropriate content. Since the Internet provides instant access to volumes of information from almost anywhere in the world, the issue became a major challenge.

The Communications Decency Act (CDA), passed in 1996, was the first attempt by the US Congress to protect children from offensive material on the Internet. The law prohibited anyone from knowingly sending or displaying offensive material on the Internet in a way that was available to children under the age of 18. Opponents claimed the law, as it was written, was impossible to enforce. They also believed the CDA violated First Amendment rights.

THE CDA AND THE SUPREME COURT

The CDA raised several legal questions. How could a sender know whether the receiver or viewer of offensive Internet material was under the age of 18? Who determines whether material is offensive? The CDA stated that material would be judged by community standards, which vary greatly throughout the country. The ACLU and other groups challenged the law in court, and the case was appealed to the Supreme Court in 1997.

> Protecting children online is really a parenting issue. If you really want to protect your children, you have to do what parents have always done: to mediate and filter what they see and hear within reason. [2]
>
> —Aric Sigman, psychologist

In *Reno v. American Civil Liberties Union*, the court ruled the CDA unconstitutional. Justice John Paul Stevens stated, "In order to deny minors access to potentially harmful speech, the CDA effectively suppresses a large

Some politicians, including Vermont senator Patrick Leahy, spoke out against the CDA after its passage.

amount of speech that adults have a constitutional right to receive and to address to one another."[3]

According to the court's decision, restricting adult Internet access was unacceptable if other means of protecting children were available. The court expressed interest in less restrictive

PROTECTING CHILDREN ONLINE

Congress passed the Child Online Protection Act (COPA) in 1998. This law made it a crime to send material that is harmful to children over the Internet for commercial purposes. It required websites to verify a visitor's age, using a credit card, for example, before granting access to adult material. After a long legal battle that involved federal courts and the Supreme Court, COPA was struck down as unconstitutional. The courts ruled COPA's standards for material that had to be hidden from open browsing were not well defined. It was not the most effective way to keep children from visiting adult websites, and it violated adults' First Amendment rights.

The Children's Internet Protection Act (CIPA) was passed in 2000. This law requires libraries and schools to place filters on their computers to prevent access to websites that are harmful to children. Failure to do so results in losing federal funding and discounts for computers. The American Library Association challenged the law because it affected libraries' ability to make information freely available to patrons. The Supreme Court upheld CIPA with the understanding that filters could easily be disabled to allow adults to access websites. Librarians will disable a filter upon request for patrons who are at least 17 years old. A library may also designate some computers without filters for adult use only. Patrons wishing to have filters disabled or to use unfiltered computers must provide proof of age and sign a form indicating the intention to use the Internet for lawful purposes.

methods of achieving the purpose of the CDA, such as content filters. Justice Stevens indicated that "user based software by which parents can prevent their children from accessing material which the *parents* believe is inappropriate will soon be widely available."[4]

HOW INTERNET CENSORSHIP WORKS

Content filtering programs became commonly used as a means of controlling access to information on the Internet. As with other forms of censorship, these filters are often the subject of

NOT JUST FOR CHILDREN

Web filters impact adults as well as children. Many corporations restrict employee access to the Internet in the workplace. One reason is to increase productivity by preventing workers from doing non-work-related activities online. Another reason is to prevent employees from viewing or circulating offensive material that may make others uncomfortable and create a hostile work environment. Some companies use web filters similar to those available for home use. Other companies use a firewall. This security system blocks some sites while allowing employees access to sites they need for their jobs. Firewall settings can be adjusted by a network administrator if an employee feels a website has been wrongfully blocked.

controversy. Those in favor of filters include parents, teachers, and librarians who are concerned about material they consider negative, dangerous, or too mature for children. They argue it is difficult, if not impossible, to supervise children's access to the Internet, and filters provide a solution to the problem.

Web filtering programs generally work through blacklists or through keyword blocking. Blacklists prevent access to a list of websites designated as undesirable. Blacklists may change over time, and updated lists are provided to users of these filters. Keyword blocking is a means of scanning a website as the user tries to visit it. The program analyzes the page for certain words that indicate the material is inappropriate. If those words are found, the filter blocks access to the site.

Courts have struck down laws that would require filtering Internet access in public libraries.

Opponents to Internet censorship point out that blacklists often block web pages that are not offensive. Keyword blocking programs cannot detect context. They often block access to acceptable websites because they detect a word that could be offensive if used in a different way. When web filters are used on public computers, such as those in a library or school, opponents raise additional concerns about censorship.

CHAPTER 6

PUBLIC LIBRARIES AND CENSORSHIP

Sharon Cook, a public library employee in Kentucky, checked out the same book over and over. Her reason for doing so eventually resulted in the loss of her job. The book was a volume of *The League of Extraordinary Gentlemen*, a graphic novel Cook considered inappropriate for children. She had filed a challenge, asking that the book be removed from the library. When that failed, she decided to take matters into her own hands. By repeatedly checking out the book, she succeeded in keeping it off the library shelf.

When a library patron placed a hold on the book, the matter became more complicated. Cook checked library records and discovered the person who had placed the hold was an 11-year-old girl. To prevent what Cook considered an offensive book from falling into the hands of a child, she removed the hold. By preventing access to the book, she violated the library's privacy policy as well as the child's First Amendment rights.

Cook believed the graphic novel was too sexually explicit for young readers at her library.

PRIVACY AND CONFIDENTIALITY

The First Amendment guarantees a person's right to freely access information. Public libraries protect privacy—a person's right to investigate a topic without having his or her interests known by others. Libraries also protect confidentiality, which exists when a library has personally identifiable information about users and keeps that information private. Such information includes records of what books a person checked out or what websites a person visited.

Most states have laws protecting the confidentiality of library records. A library's policies must conform to the specific laws of its state. The American Library Association requires all employees or volunteers who work in public libraries to "maintain an environment respectful and protective of the privacy of all users." It also advises that "everyone who collects or accesses personally identifiable information in any format has a legal and ethical obligation to protect confidentiality."[1]

To strengthen national security after the terrorist attacks of September 11, 2001, Congress passed a law known as the USA PATRIOT Act. This law gave US intelligence and police agencies broad powers, including the ability to search library patron records. Librarians, civil rights organizations, and the general public strongly objected. Section 215 of the act, sometimes called the "library provision," expired in 2015.

When Cook was fired, public opinion was divided. Some people considered her a hero for trying to protect children from indecent books. Others criticized her for imposing her own values on children by denying them the right to read freely.

DEALING WITH CHALLENGES

Because libraries serve the public, they are subject to challenges from many sources. Some come from within, as in Cook's case. Other challenges come from parents or members of religious, political, or patriotic groups who seek the removal of materials that conflict with their personal values. Librarians must honor the rights of people who challenge materials as well as protect the rights of people to read freely. Since 1967, the Office for Intellectual Freedom has helped educate librarians and the public about the importance of freedom of expression.

Most public libraries have procedures for dealing with challenges. These include a one-on-one meeting between the challenger and a librarian. A challenger may submit a written reconsideration form that is reviewed and answered by a library committee. In some cases, a challenger appeals a committee's decision to a library board or other governing body for a formal public hearing.

THE SELECTION PROCESS

The first step in responding to a challenge generally involves explaining the library's process for selecting books. Each library buys books based on its budget and available space. Within those limits, librarians select books and other resources for all people in the community. Libraries develop their own selection policies, but they follow similar guidelines. The purpose of a public library is to collect, organize, and distribute information in order to provide citizens with free access to knowledge in various forms. The materials librarians choose must represent a wide variety of subject matter and different points of view.

The school library board in Cook's county met to discuss the controversy surrounding her firing.

Some library materials are selected at the request of individuals or groups in the community. Others are chosen based on the recommendations of professional reviewers. The selection of materials does not mean the library endorses or promotes them. Librarians have a responsibility to serve the interests of the entire community. They must ensure all members of the community have access to a broad range of materials regardless of the content.

CHILDREN'S AND PARENTS' RIGHTS

Many public libraries have children's and young adult sections that provide books and other materials suited to the interests and reading abilities of those age groups. Librarians provide assistance in guiding young people to make appropriate choices. However, according to American Library Association guidelines, libraries cannot discriminate based on age or any other characteristic. The right to guide children's use of public library materials belongs to their parents. Librarians can assist parents by providing suggested book lists or reviews of materials.

According to the guidelines, librarians cannot act in place of parents by limiting access to materials. Parents have the right and the responsibility to determine their children's—and only their children's—access to library resources. In some libraries, parents

LIBRARY LABELING

Labels on library materials may be intended as an aid to users, or they may be a form of censorship. Acceptable labels, according to the American Library Association, are "viewpoint-neutral directional aids."[3] These labels help people find materials in a library. They may identify the genre of fiction books or the main category of nonfiction books.

According to American Library Association guidelines, "prejudicial" labels include movie, video, or music rating systems.[4] Labels that classify books by age, grade, or reading level are unacceptable because they may result in preventing users from accessing the full library collection. Many libraries do not follow these guidelines, instead sorting their books into children's and adult sections.

THE CHANGING ROLE OF LIBRARIES

In addition to being quiet places for reading, study, or research, many community libraries offer a large selection of programs. Adults can learn such diverse skills as how to use computer programs, how to write a novel, and how to search for records of their ancestors. Teen offerings might include essay writing, test prep, and origami. Younger children can enjoy story time or reading with specially trained therapy dogs. Adults and children can participate in read-a-thons or other contests that encourage reading as many books as possible within a specified time.

Public libraries also provide meeting rooms for book discussions or for community groups. They host a variety of workshops and sponsor speakers on topics such as health and safety. Many libraries provide free movies or concerts. Public libraries have become important community resources that are open and accessible to all—and free from censorship.

can place restrictions on their children's library cards to prevent children from checking out materials the parents find offensive.

LIBRARY BILL OF RIGHTS

Many libraries operate according to the Library Bill of Rights. This document was first adopted by the American Library Association in 1939 as a set of basic policies to guide public library services. It consists of six articles that support freedom of expression and challenge censorship.

Article V of the Library Bill of Rights is a source of controversy. It states, "A person's right to use a library should not be denied or abridged because of origin, age, background, or views."[5] Much of the debate focuses on "age." Libraries that follow a strict

Libraries often sort books based on the expected age level of the books' audience.

The addition of movies, video games, and even tablet computers to public libraries makes sorting items for age appropriateness more complicated.

interpretation of the Library Bill of Rights cannot restrict a child's use of materials.

In a 2006 survey of public libraries across the United States, about half of the libraries that responded did not allow children free access to all materials. Many of the surveyed libraries required written permission from parents for children to access nonprint

> **“** Books and other library resources should be provided for the interest, information, and enlightenment of all people of the community the library serves. Materials should not be excluded because of the origin, background, or views of those contributing to their creation. **”** [6]
>
> —**Article I of the Library Bill of Rights**

materials, such as movies, that might be considered adult content. The disagreements over age restrictions in libraries highlight these institutions' central place in the national discussion on censorship, bans, and challenges.

CHAPTER 7

MONITORING MASS MEDIA

The ACLU is committed to the protection of freedom of expression, but that does not mean always agreeing with the ideas expressed. ACLU writer Suzanne Ito stated, "The First Amendment was designed to protect offensive and unpopular speech. It is in hard cases . . . where our commitment to free speech is most tested, and most important."[1]

Brown v. Entertainment Merchants Association was one of those hard cases. California had passed a law restricting the sale or rental of violent video games to children. Representatives of the video-game industry challenged the law, and the case eventually ended up in the Supreme Court. In the 2011 decision, Justice Antonin Scalia declared that video games qualify for First Amendment protection, so the California law was unconstitutional. Justice Scalia stated, "California . . . wishes to create a wholly new category of content-based regulation that is permissible only for speech directed at children. That is unprecedented and mistaken. This country has no tradition of specially restricting children's access to depictions of violence."[2]

Violent video games, including the Grand Theft Auto series, have been the target of harsh criticism.

Four justices agreed with the majority opinion delivered by Justice Scalia. Two justices filed a separate decision in which they agreed with the majority but for different reasons. The two remaining justices filed dissenting opinions.

PROTECTING CHILDREN FROM VIOLENCE

Even people who viewed the Supreme Court decision as a victory for video games agreed not all games are appropriate for children. The First Amendment prevents the government from deciding the worth of the content. Such decisions are left to individuals or to parents. The court ruled that the video game industry's rating system was a means of assisting parents in determining what is appropriate for their children.

Rating systems or warning labels are common means of alerting people that content is inappropriate for children or disturbing to some adults. Unlike public schools or libraries, private industries can rate the content of their products. The content of movies, video games, and music is often rated to guide parents' choices for their children.

ESRB RATING SYMBOLS

The Entertainment Software Rating Board (ESRB) provides ratings for video and computer games so purchasers can make informed choices. Rating symbols on the front of a game box indicate age appropriateness. The five rating symbols range from EC (Early Childhood, ages 3 and older) to AO (Adults Only, ages 18 and older). Content descriptions on the back of a game box indicate areas of concern. These descriptions alert users to violence, strong language, or sexual themes.

MOVIE RATING SYSTEM

In 1916, the Supreme Court ruled that movies are not protected by the First Amendment, so they can be censored. Since that time, various groups have set standards to regulate content. Beginning in 1930, the Hays Code regulated the distribution of movies based on a list of rules for morality. For example, the code prohibited mocking religion, depicting illegal drug use, and showing methods of committing crimes clearly enough that they might be imitated. Following the code was mandatory for filmmakers who wanted their movies shown in American theaters. In 1934, the Roman Catholic Church set up the Legion of Decency. This group discouraged people from attending theaters that showed objectionable movies.

In 1968, the motion picture industry set up the rating system that is still in effect. Rather than approving or disapproving what audiences should see, the classifications are intended to help parents make moviegoing decisions for their family. The letter ratings have been revised over the years to the current G, PG, PG–13, R, and NC–17 classifications. Each rating also includes a short explanation as to whether the movie includes violence, drug use, nudity, or offensive language.

Movie theaters can strictly enforce ratings by refusing to sell tickets to R and NC–17 movies to unaccompanied children under the age of 17. However, theaters are not required to enforce movie ratings unless state laws require them to do so. According to a national survey in 2013, ratings enforcement by the major theater chains was at an all–time high.

MEDIA RATING SYSTEMS

Some people consider rating systems an unnecessary form of censorship. But many parents consider them a useful tool for determining what is appropriate for their children. The effectiveness of rating systems is a matter of debate.

Each industry uses its own rating system. Video game box labels indicate age appropriateness and content warnings. Movies and television shows are rated according to age groups

In 1985, Tipper Gore, wife of then senator and later vice president Al Gore, became a leading spokesperson for the Parents Music Resource Center (PMRC). This group of concerned parents criticized the explicit lyrics of popular songs. At a series of US Senate hearings, the PMRC petitioned to have parental warning labels put on records. Singers and songwriters claimed labels violated their First Amendment rights.

In an effort to resolve the issue, the recording industry agreed to identify recordings with offensive lyrics by putting a parental advisory label on them. Interviewed in 2015, Tipper Gore said, "Music is a universal language that crosses generations, race, religion, sex, and more. Never has there been more need for communication and understanding on these issues as there is today."[3]

and include specific notes about types of objectionable content. Recordings that may have offensive lyrics bear a parental advisory label. Parents may disagree with ratings based on age appropriateness because children do not mature at the same rate. Parents also have different opinions about which content is appropriate for their children.

CENSORSHIP OF TELEVISION AND RADIO

In the late 1950s, the family television show *Leave It to Beaver* was censored by the network because an episode involved showing a toilet. The two young boys in the series were trying to keep their parents from discovering a baby alligator they had ordered through the mail. They decided to hide the alligator in the toilet tank. The network finally allowed a view of the top of the tank only. The restriction on showing a toilet on television lasted well

Some stores choose not to stock music albums that have the parental advisory logo.

into the 1970s. Broadcast media—television and radio—are still subject to censorship regulations, but the determination of what is offensive has changed over time.

Federal law prohibits indecent programs on broadcast television between 6:00 a.m. and 10:00 p.m. The Federal Communications Commission (FCC) has responsibility for enforcing this law. Parents have the right and responsibility to determine appropriate viewing for their children. The Telecommunications Act, passed in 1996, provides a way for parents to block what they consider objectionable programs. The law requires a rating system that informs parents about the content of a program. The six levels of ratings range from TV-Y (suitable for all children) to TV-MA (suitable for mature audiences). Some networks also provide specific content ratings, such as L for offensive language and S for sexual situations. All television sets are required to have a V-chip, a component that allows parents to program their TV to block all shows with ratings they consider unfit in their home.

Both radio and television are regulated by a bleep censor. This tone, sometimes accompanied by a blur or box over the speaker's mouth on TV, replaces an offensive word. The bleep has been

> " The American Psychological Association urges psychologists to inform the television and film industry personnel who are responsible for violent programming, their commercial advertisers, legislators, and the general public that viewing violence in the media produces aggressive and violent behavior in children who are susceptible to such effects. " [4]
>
> —American Psychological Association

a successful way of deleting inappropriate speech. Television comedy writers sometimes purposely insert offensive words into their scripts because the bleep itself can be used as a source of humor. Live television and radio shows often operate on a seven-second delay, which allows a censor to delete objectionable words or images before they are broadcast.

FREEDOM OF THE PRESS

The news media's right to publish information free from government censorship is protected under the First Amendment. The Supreme Court has consistently ruled against prior restraint—the government's attempt to prevent publication of news. Protection from prior restraint, however, does not protect publishers from criminal penalties that may result from publishing some kinds of information. A newspaper can be convicted of libel or invasion of privacy.

FEDERAL COMMUNICATIONS COMMISSION

The FCC was created in 1934 to regulate broadcast media. Today the agency regulates telephone, radio, television, and satellite communications, and to some degree, the Internet and digital TV. The FCC cannot censor program content. It regulates material considered illegal, some aspects of children's programming, and political campaign advertising.

A person who wishes to file a complaint should provide the FCC with the date and time of the broadcast and the name of the station involved. If a television or radio station violates laws governing obscene or indecent programming, the FCC may issue a warning, impose a fine, or even revoke the station's license.

Under very limited circumstances, courts have found that prior restraint is justified. For example, reporting troop movements in a time of war could threaten national security. A Supreme Court decision noted that anything that would "surely result in direct, immediate, and irreparable damage to our Nation or its people" is not protected under the First Amendment.[5] Otherwise, news media in the United States enjoy freedom of expression not found in many other places in the world.

During World War II (1939—1945), censors in the United States prevented sensitive content from appearing in newspapers.

CHAPTER 8

CENSORSHIP AROUND THE WORLD

In April 2015, outspoken journalist Gao Yu was sentenced to seven years in a Chinese prison. The 71-year-old reporter was convicted of leaking state secrets. The secrets included a confidential Communist Party document. In it, leaders revealed a plan to ban public discussions of civil rights and freedom. The government accused Gao of sending the document to an overseas Chinese-language news organization. Gao denied the charges, and her lawyer claimed authorities forced the defendant to confess by threatening her son's safety.

For many years, Gao had been an advocate for freedom of the press in China. She was imprisoned for leaking state secrets in the 1990s, but the government never disclosed details of the case. Since Xi Jinping became president in 2013, China has jailed hundreds of activists.

According to Gao, police pressured her to dismiss her lawyers. Gao's son said prison authorities would not let the family visit her

Demonstrators in Hong Kong protested against the imprisonment of Gao Yu.

or send things to her. He also said the Chinese government warned the family not to speak publicly about the case.

Freedom of the press is often taken for granted in the United States. But suppression of news, including imprisonment of journalists, is common in many parts of the world.

A LONG HISTORY OF CENSORSHIP

Article 19 of the Universal Declaration of Human Rights states, "Everyone has the right to freedom of opinion and expression; this right includes freedom to hold opinions without interference and to seek, receive, and impart information and ideas through any media and regardless of frontiers."[1]

That document, written by the United Nations in 1948, has been violated by censors around the world. Some incidents involved individuals such as Alexandr Solzhenitsyn. The Soviet Union suppressed the works of this Nobel Prize–winning Russian author who exposed the horror of Soviet prison labor camps. Solzhenitsyn lived in exile for 20 years. British author Salman Rushdie went into hiding in 1989 when Iran's leader called for his execution. Some Muslims consider Rushdie's novel *The Satanic Verses* offensive.

Examples are not confined to the past. In 2015, the Islamist militant group ISIS burned thousands of books in Mosul, Iraq. Armed extremists destroyed books

> "There is no defense against state secret charges in China, anything the Party or the government want to label as state secrets will labeled and treated as such."[2]
>
> —Nicholas Bequelin, Amnesty International

on philosophy, science, and law, along with books of poetry and children's stories. They claimed the books promoted ideas counter to their religion. The collection included materials written centuries ago. Such extreme examples of censorship demonstrate how the destruction of a country's written heritage can also be an attack on humanity's shared culture.

DENYING FREE SPEECH TODAY

According to the Committee to Protect Journalists (CPJ), imprisonment is the most effective method for censoring reporters today. In 2014, governments worldwide jailed more than 200 journalists.[3] More than half of them were charged with crimes against their governments. To suppress information, these governments also restricted journalists' movements and kept out foreign reporters.

CHARLIE HEBDO

On January 7, 2015, two heavily armed attackers forced their way into the offices of *Charlie Hebdo*, a weekly newspaper in Paris, France, and killed ten members of the staff. Two policemen were also killed, and at least 11 other people were wounded. The attack was carried out by Muslim terrorists who shouted, "We have avenged the Prophet Muhammad!"[4]

Since its introduction in 1970, *Charlie Hebdo* has frequently been controversial. The newspaper has a long history of mocking religions, often through cartoons. In 2006, it reprinted controversial cartoons of the prophet Muhammad that had originally appeared in a Danish newspaper. Images of the prophet are offensive to some Muslims. French law prohibits speech that "insults, defames, or incites hatred, discrimination, or violence."[5] The editors of *Charlie Hebdo* were warned but never censored for their views.

The editorial director of *Charlie Hebdo* rejected any suggestion to tone down the publication's satirical approach to avoid criticism. The newspaper made fun of Muslims, Jews, and Christians. Politicians were also favorite targets of ridicule. A letter published by the staff of *Charlie Hebdo* and its supporters stated, "We, writers, journalists, intellectuals, call for resistance to religious totalitarianism and for the promotion of freedom, equal opportunity, and secular values for all."[6]

People around the world showed their support for *Charlie Hebdo* and free speech in the wake of the attacks.

Some people believed the newspaper could have avoided the attack by softening its political and religious views. Others believed the attack was an assault on freedom everywhere. At massive marches and on online message boards, the words Je suis Charlie, or "I am Charlie," were posted to show support for freedom of expression.[7]

Other government tactics against the press include raiding newspaper offices, threatening advertisers, and charging reporters with crimes such as drug possession. In some places, journalists' relatives are told they could lose their jobs. In the most severe cases, journalists are abducted, held captive, and killed.

CENSORSHIP IN THE INFORMATION AGE

In the past, governments suppressed freedom of expression by monitoring and altering the content of print materials, news broadcasts, or movies. This method ensured people had access only to information the government considered acceptable. Today, governments have found other ways to monitor and control the flow of information.

In 1993, Internet pioneer John Gilmore said, "The Net interprets censorship as damage and routes around it."[8] But governments found ways to use the Internet to expand the scope of censorship. Hungary, for example, used fines and taxes to disadvantage critical media and placed state advertising only in

COMMITTEE TO PROTECT JOURNALISTS

In 1981, a group of US correspondents decided they could not ignore the plight of other journalists who put themselves in danger to report the news. They formed a committee of journalists around the world to take action. The Committee to Protect Journalists (CPJ) documents cases and publishes reports. It makes the public aware of abuses against the press. CPJ provides support to journalists who are censored, threatened, jailed, or kidnapped. It organizes protests and works to bring about change to ensure freedom of the press around the world.

> **If you want to dominate an enemy, you have to neutralize or negate them; take away any sort of information that . . . supports the memory of whatever system was operative before the conquest.** [9]
>
> —Rebecca Knuth, professor and author

media outlets that supported government policies. Russia blocked media outlets and limited foreign investment in Russian media. In Venezuela, the government gained influence over the independent media by purchasing the country's newspapers through anonymous buyers. An amendment to Turkey's Internet law gave the government authority to block websites or content to protect national security and to prevent crime. Journalists who criticized the government were subjected to tax investigations and huge fines.

China openly cracked down on media coverage but also censored in ways that were not made public. To control the flow of information, the Chinese government used cyberattacks on foreign newspapers, withdrew advertising, and fired reporters. Censorship in the information age has become a battle between governments that seek to repress freedom of expression and courageous citizens who are willing to oppose them.

THE TOP TEN LIST

Eritrea and North Korea headed the top ten list of most censored countries in 2015. The list is compiled each year by the Committee to Protect Journalists (CPJ). It is based on research into government restrictions on freedom of expression.

The government of Eritrea launched a campaign to crush independent journalism by creating a hostile environment for reporters. Eritrea was Africa's worst jailer of journalists. Most of them were not tried in court or even charged with a crime. Reporters lived in constant fear, and many left the country rather than risk arrest. The government limited public access to outside information. Eritrea had the lowest rate of cell phone ownership in the world in 2015, and less than 1 percent of the people had Internet access.

North Korea prohibited almost all access to the Internet. The government allowed some schools and other institutions to use a tightly controlled and filtered computer network. Less than 10 percent of the population had cell phones. Foreign reporters were allowed into the country as long as they were supervised and guided by North Korean officials, but the government kept tight control on the media. Almost everything in the country's newspapers, periodicals, and broadcasts came from the Korean Central News Agency. News reports and historical records were edited to remove photos of the leader's uncle, who had been executed for treason in 2013.

According to CPJ's annual prison census, many other countries on the list of top ten most censored countries were also among the worst jailers worldwide. China (number eight on the list) imprisoned 44 journalists in 2015. Saudi Arabia (number three) dealt harshly with criticism of its leadership. Relying on a

Free speech in North Korean society is harshly restricted, and citizens are subject to intensive propaganda in posters, television, and other media.

MORE THAN HALF THE WORLD

In 2015, almost half the world had Internet access. That means more than half the world's people—an estimated 4.4 billion—remained offline. The majority of those people lived in China, India, and the United States. According to a study in 2014, China led the world in cell phone users, but more than half its population was not online. More than a billion people in India were not Internet users, and 50 million people in the United States did not use the Internet.[11]

The reasons why people remained disconnected include a lack of technology infrastructure or high cost. But mobile Internet on smartphones provided access to fill some of these gaps.

2009 law that prohibits any reporting that encourages dissent, Ethiopia (number four) jailed 17 journalists in 2015. Vietnam (number six) often put journalists under government surveillance to make sure they did not report on certain issues.[10]

SUPPRESSION OF THE INTERNET

China, the country with the world's most Internet users, launched a major crackdown against freedom of expression in 2014. The government maintained the so-called Great Firewall to block access to unacceptable content, including foreign news sites. Chinese authorities monitored users' online activities and suppressed dissent. The combination of technological censorship and the imprisonment of violators succeeded in suppressing the Internet.

Internet usage in China, including at Internet cafés, is closely monitored and heavily censored.

Though Google continues to operate in China, many of its services and products are restricted or outright blocked there.

In 2015, Internet access was highly restricted in many Communist countries, including Cuba. Despite outside investment to provide the Internet there, only a small percentage of the population had access. Iran had one of the toughest Internet censorship policies, with millions of websites blocked. Azerbaijan extended its criminal laws to include any criticism of the government on social media, with a six-month prison sentence for offenders. As a result of censorship, only a small minority of the world's people enjoyed open access to information on the Internet in 2015.

CENSORSHIP AND THE ECONOMY

China's censorship of the Internet had global economic consequences. Companies in the United States and elsewhere that were involved in online communication or digital trade suffered economic setbacks due to China's policies. For example, in 2012 Chinese authorities blocked the *New York Times* website to censor an investigative report into the wealth of one of China's leaders. The *Times* lost revenue and had to renegotiate agreements with many advertisers.

Foreign companies that do business within China are responsible for censoring content to meet Chinese standards. China was the second-largest source of revenue for the US electronics company Apple. To avoid having to develop a censorship system, Apple chose to disable its news app in China. Chinese companies also suffer from China's unexpected policy changes. Sina Corporation, a media company that serves Chinese communities around the world, has monitoring and censorship systems. When the Chinese government suddenly revoked two of Sina's trade licenses, the company's stock dropped, impacting investors around the world.

CHAPTER 9

AN ONGOING ISSUE

Censorship may be imposed by governments, by religious groups, by political groups, or by individuals who are trying to protect children. Censorship can be subtle or violent. Regardless of the reason or the method, censorship always involves a denial of someone's right to freedom of expression, and it is an ongoing issue. Efforts to fight censorship are also ongoing, both at the international level and in local communities.

MOVEMENT TOWARD GLOBAL FREEDOM OF EXPRESSION

According to the United Nations Special Rapporteur on the Promotion and Protection of the Right to Freedom of Opinion and Expression, the Internet has opened new possibilities for the realization of the right to freedom of expression. It also has the potential to be misused to harm others.

The United Nations and other international organizations work with governments to combat censorship and provide global freedom of expression through traditional media as well as on the Internet. By 2015, several governments around the world, including

Around the world, censorship is often seen as a direct threat to democracy.

Estonia, France, and Costa Rica, recognized Internet access as a human right. India sponsored public kiosks for Internet access. Brazil offered subsidies for purchasing computers. Jillian C. York, Director for International Freedom of Expression at the Electronic Frontier Foundation, was encouraged by this progress. She stated, "The one thing that gives me hope though is the growing movement for digital rights happening around the world."[1]

SUCCESS STORIES ON THE HOME FRONT

Other victories for freedom of expression took place much closer to home. The following success

> By vastly expanding the capacity of individuals to enjoy their right to freedom of opinion and expression, which is an 'enabler' of other human rights, the Internet . . . contributes to the progress of humankind as a whole.[3]
>
> —Frank La Rue,
> Special Rapporteur

stories are among many that took place in local communities around the United States.

In 2013, the principal of Trumbull High School in Trumbull, Connecticut, canceled plans for the musical *Rent*. He called the play too controversial, even though students were to perform a school edition from which many objectionable parts had been removed. Students fought the decision by starting a petition, which eventually gained support from approximately 1,500 people.[4] They also posted information on Facebook. In view of the community support and media coverage, the principal reconsidered, and the show went on.

A Glen Ellyn, Illinois, school district banned Stephen Chbosky's *The Perks of Being a Wallflower* in middle school libraries in 2013. Students, parents, and teachers reacted by rallying the community to support the book. Some enterprising students also asked children's author Judy Blume to participate in a video, which they sent to the school board

JUDY BLUME

Judy Blume is an award-winning author whose books have sold more than 80 million copies worldwide.[5] She is also one of the most frequently challenged authors of recent decades. Her books for children and teens deal with real-life issues such as sex, drugs, and homosexuality. Blume is an active defender of the right to read. In 2013, she joined Glen Ellyn, Illinois, students in their efforts to reinstate *The Perks of Being a Wallflower* in their school. Blume was attending a book fair where she received a literary award when the students asked for her help. The author not only participated in a video the students made, but also donated her $5,000 prize money to the NCAC on their behalf.[6]

to protest the ban. The book was reinstated.

ACTION PLANS

National organizations, such as the NCAC and the American Library Association, work to protect freedom of expression. These groups promote not only the freedom to exercise one's own rights but also the responsibility to defend the rights of others. They encourage individuals to become involved in the defense of freedom of expression.

The first requirement in any action plan is to become informed. People who defend the right to read, as well as people who challenge books, have a responsibility to read and understand the materials. Online book reviews provide useful information, and news publications generally cover different viewpoints about an issue. Public meetings of school boards,

School board meetings are one of the key locations in which book challenges are discussed.

The ever-widening role of modern libraries is likely to spur continuing discussions about book bans, book challenges, and censorship.

library boards, and parent-teacher associations provide forums for discussion.

Challenges to books are complaints that deserve consideration and resolution. The NCAC recommends that schools and libraries have policies in place to deal with challenges. Banning is a form of censorship—a denial of someone's rights—and should not be tolerated. The examples of success stories indicate how individuals can fight censorship. An action plan includes mobilizing the community, using social media and the press, and seeking support from others who are committed to preserving freedom of expression.

> **Recognizing that others have different views . . . and that their views are entitled to the same respect and protection as your own is a form of tolerance required of all in a pluralistic society.**[8]
>
> —**National Coalition Against Censorship**

Freedom of expression, protected by law, is rare in a world where many people can be imprisoned for their views. Neil Gaiman, award-winning English writer and free-speech defender, warned against taking the First Amendment for granted. He said coming to the United States was "like visiting a place where people had the most valuable, wonderful, perfect thing in the world and just didn't value it."[7]

ESSENTIAL FACTS

MAJOR EVENTS

» In 1939, the Library Bill of Rights established basic policies that supported freedom of expression and challenged censorship.

» In 1968, the motion picture industry established a rating system for movies.

» In 1978, a federal court ruled that a school board cannot edit or remove books from the library based on objections to language or theme.

» In 1988, the Supreme Court supported a school's right to censor a student newspaper for the purpose of protecting other students' rights.

» In 2000, the Children's Internet Protection Act required libraries and schools to place filters on computers to prevent access to websites that are harmful to children.

» In 2014, China launched a major crackdown against freedom of expression.

KEY PLAYERS

» The American Library Association promotes the improvement of library and information services to enhance learning and ensure equal access to information for everyone.

» The National Coalition Against Censorship educates people about censorship and provides strategies to protect freedom of thought and expression.

» The Committee to Protect Journalists promotes worldwide freedom of the press and defends the right of journalists to report the news without fear of censorship or violence.

» The American Civil Liberties Union challenges censorship laws and provides legal assistance to those seeking to preserve freedom of speech.

IMPACT ON SOCIETY

Censorship impacts what people say, what they write, what they hear, and what they see. Whether imposed by governments, by religious and political groups, or by well-meaning individuals, censorship involves a denial of someone's right to freedom of expression. In the United States, courts have interpreted the right to freedom of expression guaranteed by the First Amendment. The United Nations and other international groups seek to protect this right worldwide. In the information age, censorship continues to threaten the potential for global communication and the free exchange of ideas.

QUOTE

"A book worthless to me may convey something of value to my neighbor. In the free society to which our Constitution has committed us, it is for each to choose for himself."

—US Supreme Court Justice Potter Stewart

GLOSSARY

BAN
To remove a book from a library or classroom to prevent its use.

BOWDLERIZE
To edit literature by removing parts the editor considers inappropriate.

CENSORSHIP
The act of imposing values on others by limiting what they may read, write, hear, or see.

CHALLENGE
An attempt to remove a book from a library or classroom or to restrict its use.

CONFIDENTIALITY
The protection of personal information.

CONTROVERSY
A public debate concerning a matter of opinion.

CYBERATTACK
An attempt to damage or destroy a computer network or system.

DISCRIMINATION
Unfair treatment of other people, usually because of race, age, or gender.

FIREWALL

Computer hardware or software that blocks unauthorized users.

FUNDAMENTAL

A central principle on which something is based.

LIBEL

A published false statement that is damaging to a person's reputation.

OBSCENE

Offensive or disgusting by accepted standards of decency.

PREJUDICE

An opinion that is not based on reason or actual experience.

PRIOR RESTRAINT

A government's attempt to prevent publication of news.

PRIVACY

Free from public attention.

RACISM

Inferior treatment of a person or group of people based on race.

SUPPRESSION

Preventing the development, action, or expression of an idea.

ADDITIONAL RESOURCES

SELECTED BIBLIOGRAPHY

"About Banned & Challenged Books." *American Library Association*. American Library Association, n.d. Web. 28 Jan. 2016.

Foerstel, Herbert N. *Banned in the U.S.A.: A Reference Guide to Book Censorship in Schools and Public Libraries*. Westport, CT: Greenwood, 2002. Print.

"The First Amendment in Schools: A Resource Guide." *National Coalition Against Censorship*. National Coalition Against Censorship, n.d. Web. 28 Jan. 2016.

FURTHER READINGS

Capek, Michael. *Religion and Free Speech*. Minneapolis, MN: Abdo, 2016. Print.

Lusted, Marcia Amidon. *Tinker v. Des Moines: The Right to Protest in Schools*. Minneapolis, MN: Abdo, 2013. Print.

WEBSITES

To learn more about Essential Library of the Information Age, visit **booklinks.abdopublishing.com**. These links are routinely monitored and updated to provide the most current information available.

FOR MORE INFORMATION

For more information on this subject, contact or visit the following organizations:

First Amendment Center/Newseum

555 Pennsylvania Avenue
Washington, DC 20001
202-292-6288
http://www.firstamendmentcenter.org

The First Amendment Center works to build understanding of core freedoms through education, information, and entertainment. Its website features daily news updates and reports about US Supreme Court cases involving the First Amendment as well as analysis of free expression, press freedom, and religious liberty issues.

National Coalition Against Censorship (NCAC)

19 Fulton Street, Suite 407
New York, NY 10038
212-807-6222
http://www.ncac.org

The National Coalition Against Censorship promotes freedom of thought, inquiry, and expression and opposes censorship in all its forms. Its website lists many ways to help protect freedom of expression.

SOURCE NOTES

CHAPTER 1. WHAT IS CENSORSHIP?

1. Barbara Conaty. "City of Thieves." *Library Journal*. Library Journal, 1 Apr. 2008. Web. 6 Nov. 2015.

2. "Charter School's Book Censorship is a 'Kind of Literary Fraud.'" *National Coalition Against Censorship*. National Coalition Against Censorship, 24 Sept. 2015. Web. 29 Sept. 2015.

3. "Thomas Bowdler." *Biography*. A&E Television Networks, n.d. Web. 19 Sept. 2015.

4. "*Right to Read Defense Committee of Chelsea v. School Committee of the City of Chelsea*." *Leagle*. Leagle, 1978. Web. 2 Mar. 2016.

5. "Mission & History." *National Coalition Against Censorship*. National Coalition Against Censorship, n.d. Web. 30 Sept. 2015.

6. "Bill of Rights." *Charters of Freedom*. National Archives, n.d. Web. 2 Mar. 2016.

7. "*Right to Read Defense Committee of Chelsea v. School Committee of the City of Chelsea*." *Leagle*. Leagle, 1978. Web. 2 Mar. 2016.

8. Ibid.

9. Ibid.

10. "Charter School's Book Censorship is a 'Kind of Literary Fraud.'" *National Coalition Against Censorship*. National Coalition Against Censorship, 24 Sept. 2015. Web. 29 Sept. 2015.

CHAPTER 2. BANNED!

1. Judith Miller. "History's Greatest Book Burners." *Daily Beast*. Daily Beast, 9 Sept. 2010. Web. 1 Oct. 2015.

2. Molly Guptill Manning. *When Books Went to War*. New York: Houghton Mifflin Harcourt, 2014. Print. 48.

3. Neil Miller. *Banned in Boston: The Watch and Ward Society's Crusade against Books, Burlesque, and the Social Evil*. Boston, MA: Beacon, 2010. Print.

4. "Top Ten Frequently Challenged Book Lists of the 21st Century." *American Library Association*. American Library Association, n.d. Web. 2 Oct. 2015.

5. Elizabeth Kennedy. "They're Burning Books Again." *About.com*. About. com, n.d. Web. 3 Oct. 2015.

6. "'Satanic' Harry Potter Books Burnt." *BBC News*. BBC News, 31 Dec. 2001. Web. 3 Oct. 2015.

7. "Books that Shaped America: Exhibition Overview." *Library of Congress*. Library of Congress, n.d. Web. 2 Oct. 2015.

8. Herbert N. Foerstel. *Banned in the U.S.A: A Reference Guide to Book Censorship in Schools and Public Libraries*. Westport, CT: Greenwood, 2002. Print. 156.

9. Ibid. 139.

CHAPTER 3. CENSORSHIP IN SCHOOLS

1. "Number of Instructional Days/ Hours in the School Year." *Education Commission of the States*. Education Commission of the States, Aug. 2011. Web. 4 Oct. 2015.

2. "*Tinker v. Des Moines Independent Community School District*." *Cornell University Law School*. Cornell, 1969. Web. 4 Oct. 2015.

3. "The Great Textbook War." *American RadioWorks*. American Public Media, n.d. Web. 21 Sept. 2015.

4. "*Tinker v. Des Moines Independent Community School District*." *Cornell University Law School*. Cornell, 1969. Web. 4 Oct. 2015.

5. Ibid.

6. David R. Wheeler. "Do Students Still Have Free Speech in School?" *Atlantic*. Atlantic, 7 Apr. 2014. Web. 5 Oct. 2015.

7. "*Bethel School District v. Fraser*." *Leagle*. Leagle, 1986. Web. 2 Mar. 2016.

CHAPTER 4. BOTH SIDES OF THE ISSUE

1. "Excerpt from Plato's *Republic*, Books II & III." *University of Connecticut*. University of Connecticut, n.d. Web. 1 Oct. 2015.

2. Kathy Durbin. "Books Under Fire." *Teaching Tolerance*. Southern Poverty Law Center, Spring 2005. Web. 18 Oct. 2015.

3. Ibid.

4. Michael Moynihan. "The Politics of Literature: An Interview with Nobel Laureate Mario Vargas Llosa." *Daily Beast*. Daily Beast, 10 Oct. 2013. Web. 21 Sept. 2015.

5. Mario Vargas Llosa. "Why Literature?" *New Republic*. New Republic, 14 May 2001. Web. 7 Oct. 2015.

6. Sara Yasin. "In Praise of Malala Yousafzai." *Index on Censorship*. Index on Censorship, 12 July 2013. Web. 23 Oct. 2015.

7. "*Ginzburg et al v. United States*." *Leagle*. Leagle, 1966. Web. 2 Mar. 2016.

8. Ashley Lauren Samsa. "A Modern Look at Banned Books." *Teaching Tolerance*. Southern Poverty Law Center, 25 Sept. 2013. Web. 17 Oct. 2015.

9. "*Pierce v. Society of Sisters*." *Leagle*. Leagle, 1925. Web. 2 Mar. 2016.

10. "Understanding the Parental Rights Amendment." *Parental Rights Organization*. Parental Rights Organization, n.d. Web. 7 Oct. 2015.

11. Ibid.

12. David Daley. "Making a Case for Censorship." *Courant*. Courant, 2 Sept. 1999. Web. 9 Nov. 2015.

SOURCE NOTES CONT.

CHAPTER 5. THE INTERNET AND FREEDOM OF EXPRESSION

1. "Internet Lives Stats." *Internet Live Stats*. Internet Live Stats, 2 Mar. 2016. Web. 2 Mar. 2016.

2. Aric Sigman. "What Children Need Is Censorship." *Guardian*. Guardian, 11 Nov. 2008. Web. 30 Sept. 2015.

3. *"Reno v. American Civil Liberties Union."* Leagle. Leagle, 1997. Web. 2 Mar. 2016.

4. Ibid.

CHAPTER 6. PUBLIC LIBRARIES AND CENSORSHIP

1. "Privacy: An Interpretation of the Library Bill of Rights." *American Library Association*. American Library Association, n.d. Web. 17 Oct. 2015.

2. Gordon M. Conable. "Public Libraries and Intellectual Freedom." *American Library Association*. American Library Association, n.d. Web. 21 Sept. 2015.

3. "Questions and Answers on Labeling and Rating Systems." *American Library Association*. American Library Association, n.d. Web. 12 Oct. 2015.

4. Ibid.

5. "Library Bill of Rights." *American Library Association*. American Library Association, n.d. Web. 12 Sept. 2015.

6. Ibid.

CHAPTER 7. MONITORING MASS MEDIA

1. Suzanne Ito. "Protecting Outrageous, Offensive Speech." *ACLU*. ACLU, 6 Oct. 2010. Web. 13 Oct. 2015.

2. *"Brown v. Entertainment Merchants Association."* Leagle. Leagle, 2011. Web. 2 Mar. 2016.

3. Kory Grow. "Tipper Gore Reflects on PMRC 30 Years Later." *Rolling Stone*. Rolling Stone, 14 Sept. 2015. Web. 13 Oct. 2015.

4. "Violence in Mass Media." *Resolution on Television Violence*. American Psychological Association, n.d. Web. 13 Oct. 2015.

5. Douglas E. Lee. "Prior Restraint." *First Amendment Center*. First Amendment Center, 13 Sept. 2002. Web. 14 Oct. 2015.

CHAPTER 8. CENSORSHIP AROUND THE WORLD

1. "Universal Declaration of Human Rights." *United Nations*. United Nations, n.d. Web. 15 Oct. 2015.

2. Steven Jiang. "China Jails Prominent Journalist Gao Yu for Leaking State Secrets." *CNN*. CNN, 17 Apr. 2015. Web. 14 Oct. 2015.

3. "2014 Prison Census: 221 Journalists Jailed Worldwide." *Committee to Protect Journalists*. Committee to Protect Journalists, 1 Dec. 2014. Web. 2 Mar. 2016.

4. "*Charlie Hebdo* Attack: Three Days of Terror." *BBC News*. BBC News, 14 Jan. 2015. Web. 15 Oct. 2015.

5. Jonathan Turley. "The Biggest Threat to French Free Speech Isn't Terrorism. It's the Government." *Washington Post*. Washington Post, 8 Jan. 2015. Web. 15 Oct. 2015.

6. Megan Gibson. "The Provocative History of French Weekly Newspaper *Charlie Hebdo*." *Time*. Time, 7 Jan. 2015. Web. 15 Oct. 2015.

7. "The *Charlie Hebdo* Massacre in Paris." *New York Times*. New York Times, 7 Jan. 2015. Web. 15 Oct. 2015.

8. "Boing Boing's Guide to Defeating Censorware." *Boing Boing*. Boing Boing, n.d. Web. 2 Mar. 2016.

9. Jeffrey Kastner. "The Past Is in Flames: An Interview with Rebecca Knuth." *Cabinet*. Cabinet, Fall/Winter 2003. Web. 15 Oct. 2015.

10. Catherine Taibi. "These Are the Most Censored Countries in the World." *Huffington Post*. Huffington Post, 21 Apr. 2015. Web. 13 Oct. 2015.

11. Tim Fitzsimons. "Why 4.4 Billion People Still Don't Have Internet Access." *NPR*. NPR, 2 Oct. 2014. Web. 19 Oct. 2015.

CHAPTER 9. AN ONGOING ISSUE

1. Julia Hudson. "Online Censorship: What Does the Future Hold for Our Ideas?" *Virgin*. Virgin, 24 Feb. 2015. Web. 8 Nov. 2015.

2. "Special Procedures of the Human Rights Council." *United Nations*. United Nations, n.d. Web. 23 Oct. 2015.

3. "Human Rights in Cyberspace." *Australian Human Rights Commission*. Australian Human Rights Commission, n.d. Web. 16 Oct. 2015.

4. Acacia O'Connor. "The Curtain Lifts on Rent in Connecticut after Controversy." *National Coalition Against Censorship*. National Coalition Against Censorship, 26 Mar. 2014. Web. 10 Nov. 2015.

5. Alison Flood. "Judy Blume: 'I Thought This Is America: We Don't Ban Books. But Then We Did.'" *Guardian*. Guardian, 11 July 2014. Web. 11 Nov. 2015.

6. Stacy St. Clair. "Glen Ellyn Board Listens to Blume, Reinstates YA Novel." *Chicago Tribune*. Chicago Tribune, 12 June 2013. Web. 10 Nov. 2015.

7. "Free Speech Matters: NCAC's 40th Anniversary Celebration." *National Coalition Against Censorship*. National Coalition Against Censorship, 3 Nov. 2014. Web. 10 Nov. 2015.

8. "Fight Censorship." *National Coalition Against Censorship*. National Coalition Against Censorship, n.d. Web. 10 Nov. 2015.

INDEX

ABOUT THE AUTHOR

Carolee Laine is an educator and children's writer. She has written social studies textbooks and other educational materials as well as passages for statewide assessments. She enjoys learning through researching and writing nonfiction books for young readers. Laine lives in the Chicago, Illinois, suburbs.